Meditation, Mind and Body

A 12-Week Meditation Course
for Mentored or Self Study

Jivan Amara

Copyright © 2018 Jivan Amara
All rights reserved.

This publication is designed to provide general information regarding the subject matter covered. Nothing in this book is meant to be portrayed as medical advice, counseling, or therapy.

http://meditate.jivanamara.net/

Introduction

There are a countless number of meditation books out there, why another? I find there's still a widespread misconception that meditation is primarily a method to stop thought and meditation is often presented in a religious context which can make it difficult for a modern person to digest. I'd like to present a more complete view of meditation in a way that references some of the forms it has taken in different spiritual traditions but doesn't require you to adopt the beliefs of those traditions without evidence. I'd like to encourage an attitude of spiritual practices as an exploration, an investigation, and even research.

I hope that this will result in people more easily able to share their inner discoveries rather than losing them behind the boundaries drawn by different faiths. The world is changing dramatically around us and in order to apply our spiritual insights during this change our understanding and spiritual perspective needs to keep pace with it.

One of those changes is a failing of hierarchical belief structures analogous to a king ruling a country. This sort of "belief dictatorship" has no place in a human endeavor where truth is valued. These structures also often result in belief propagated blindly. Over time what may have once been a valuable insight may be misconstrued or simply no longer relevant. When the reason for adopting a perspective or practice is not passed on we lose the ability to determine if it is still relevant or valuable.

In keeping with an attitude of discovery, I want to present meditation as something for you to experience and verify first-hand. Using the analogy of meditation as research, your laboratory is your experience and the instruments of your experiments are focus and subtlety of mind, which you will help to form through these practices. While I give some potential effects to look for so that uncertain beginners have some measuring stick to provide themselves with feedback, I'd like to emphasize that it's your first-hand evidence that's ultimately of value. This kind of experiential evidence allows you a certainty and depth of understanding that second-hand knowledge can never provide.

This book is arranged to be used both as a self-study course and as a mentored course. The most important elements to bring to it are a genuine interest and steady commitment. I'd like to encourage the independence of those drawn to self-study, but it's important to acknowledge that there is a great deal of value that supports like a meditation group and an experienced mentor can provide.

I'm not very interested in promulgating beliefs, but that includes both the belief that something is true and the belief that something is false. The attitude I'd like you to take into this is one of open-minded skepticism. Be open and attentive to the practices and very honest about what occurs during that time. Notice any clear trend during the week you undertake each practice. If you try and find nothing, let that be what you carry forward.

If you have any questions, I can be reached at:
MeditationCourse@JivanAmara.net

Additional copies of this book can be purchased at:
meditate.jivanamara.net/buy-book

You can subscribe to mentoring at:
meditate.jivanamara.net/subscribe-to-mentoring

Table of Contents

Before We Begin...1

Week 1: Scoping Yourself Out...5
Week 2: Starting to Practice, Dealing With Thinking..............9
Week 3: Bringing Attention to the Body...............................13
Week 4: Emotion & More Deeply Into the Body..................17
Week 5: More to the Body...21
Week 6: Using Movement to Uncover Hidden Sensations...23
Week 7: More Deeply Into the Breath, Part I........................25
Week 8: More Deeply Into the Breath, Part II.......................29
Week 9: Where Do They Come From?.................................31
Week 10: Energy Channels in the Body...............................33
Week 11: What Am I Really?...37
Week 12: Back to Fundamentals..41

Appendix I - Paths Forward..43

About the Author..46

Before We Begin
The 3 + 3 Commitment

Meditation is such a deeply healing and transformative practice, I'm happy you're taking the time and attention to give it a real opportunity in your life. Those possibilities include peace, insight, connection, among others. Through this entire course I want you to remember first and foremost that the highest authority here is your own experience.

It takes some commitment to realize these benefits. We wouldn't expect to pick up a guitar and play masterfully in a week, how much more so for the powerful inner experiences that saints and sages speak of? That said, it also shouldn't require undiscerning faith; the benefits should be clear enough that it takes little effort to continue, just a recognition of the value you find and a little bit of discipline to make time to "cultivate your garden". I ask that you commit at least 10 minutes, and ideally 20 minutes after waking and before sleeping for three months.

If three months is too much now, you can make a commitment for three weeks and extend it to three months provided you see some benefit. Three weeks isn't much but should be enough to get a small taste of what three months could potentially bring you. If you don't see any benefit during this time, explore another direction. I expect that if you follow through on your commitment that's an unlikely outcome and after you've had a taste of what can come from this, a full three month commitment will show you deeply where these practices will fit in your life and some of the subtle and powerful ways they can help you navigate and explore. Enjoy this inner journey; it can change your life in unexpected ways.

Meditation, Mind and Body

> Each chapter has a suggested journaling topic. These are optional exercises and you are encouraged to do them if you can make the time. They will be particularly helpful looking back after the end of the course to see what you've discovered and to help you choose the best path forward for your practice.

I encourage you to avoid reading ahead. Focus on the instructions and suggestions for the week you're on and wait to read the following week's material until the current week is complete. If you are interested in meditating for longer or more frequently, please don't hesitate.

What should you expect? There are a lot of experiences that arise in meditation; for those uncertain and doing the three week trial commitment, things to watch for are a fresh sense of peace, of wellbeing, either during your practice or unexpectedly during your day. Outwardly this can appear as a sense of ease in your daily activities or a sense of flowing through your activities with a distance that makes what would be chaotic or frustrating circumstances have notably less effect on your inner state. In a three week trial there may be only a single glimpse of one of these experiences, but it will make clear what is in store with a renewed commitment for three months.

Now the bad news...A steady practice will build an energy or potential in your being. As that energy builds the extra energy available starts flowing along lines that previously lay dormant. This will power both sweet and uncomfortable experiences. At some point in your practice you will open up a peaceful and clear space full of life and potential. When this happens, uncomfortable material you've been avoiding either through suppression or distraction will flow into this space for attention. This is the reason I emphasize making a commitment, so that these uncomfortable experiences don't immediately turn you away. What you'll likely find is riding them out clears up old blocks or pain and opens new freedom within you. A new understanding of the issue may arise to help you to avoid recreating the problem in the future. Use a gentle discipline to stay present to them. In all, do your best not to get attached to the sweet experiences that arise and don't avoid the uncomfortable experiences. This will prevent the energy of the practice from dissipating and you will feel it build, both on your cushion and in your life.

Examples of common uncomfortable states that you may experience:

Uncertainty: If you're new to meditation, you may spend some time wondering if there's any real value to it. Invite these thoughts to return at the end of your commitment for genuine consideration.

Self-Doubt: You may conclude that it's something wrong with you that has prevented some sort of validating experience. There's no need to engage these thoughts now, revisit them at the end of your commitment.

Fear: There is a very real possibility of unfamiliar experiences arising. This can be both a source of excitement and of fear. In general expect an object of fear (i.e. a bear) and the fear itself. Be sure to give attention to the fear itself more than the object of the fear. If fear becomes too intense, take a break. If it continues to be too intense after a break, find a mentor.

Vulnerability: Life's circumstances often lead to us building psychological protections that give us a sense of strength or control. Seeing and feeling the vulnerability beneath them can be uncomfortable. Stay with the experience & provide yourself with support by not encouraging any harsh reactions that may come up during the experience.

Sadness: It's not fun and is usually avoided socially, so we tend to pack it away. Expect to find that storage locker at some point in your practice.

Anger: Much like sadness, it's often socially unacceptable and gets packed away. Do your best to stay with it without trying to manipulate it in any way. If you feel you must express it, find an option that you won't regret; like a pillow assault or time on the heavy bag at your local boxing club.

Week 1
Why Meditate? Scoping Yourself Out

This week we're not going to start meditating yet, but take a look at the motivations and influences that have brought you to meditate.

I'm going to ask you that during the time you've committed in the morning and evening to write about what you feel is pushing you to try this or what you are hoping will happen. A perfectly clear answer is not necessary; just do your best to put words to what you find moving you.

If you do get a fairly clear answer to this inquiry, I'd like you to use your imagination to play out the scenario you've seen. Lay down or sit comfortably with your eyes closed and relax. Let go of all your day-to-day concerns and immerse yourself in your imagination. If it is a particular impulse pushing you, use your imagination to follow the impulse and see where it goes. If it is a clear result or aim, immerse yourself in that situation and fill out any additional details of that success or completion. Once you've done this, check what is different in your thoughts, in your feelings, in your body. What you'll likely find is a more significant, more subtle desire beneath the surface, unrecognized. Below are some examples of how this can unfold.

> *"I want to meditate so I'm more effective at work in order to forward my career."*
> I imagine meditation providing the boost I need and myself enjoying my senior position. I look inside and feel the satisfaction of accomplishment. The underlying desire here is accomplishment.

> *"I want to get away from all the frustration at work"*
> I imagine myself in a beautiful place with no work responsibilities, such as a forest, beach, cafe, pub, or club. I look inside and I feel peace. The real desire here is for peace.

> *"I want to develop spiritually."*
> I imagine myself as a developed spiritual being and look inside. I feel that I'm being honored. The real desire is to be honored.

There are no right answers in this process, only true answers. In doing this we get clarity about what we're truly after, allowing us to be open to receiving it in more ways than our current expectations would allow, or to leave it behind if it doesn't ring true for us.

This process will often reveal a wound that needs attention. From the examples above: I may desire to accomplish more something because right now I'm feeling ineffective, powerless. I may desire to feel honored because right now I'm feeling insignificant, unworthy.

When you've got a glimpse of the underlying motive it is often useful to repeat the process starting from there for even greater depth and clarity. If you're feeling pretty steady in your emotional life the process can also be done with any fears that you are facing. The critical factors to success in this exercise are honesty and taking the time to really fill out details in your imagination.

Each day your work from the previous day and events from life will likely bring more to light. When underlying desires are fairly clear look over what you've collected and ask yourself a couple of questions; first, of the underlying desires do these feel right for me? It's good to check-in like this, as things we've set as desirable earlier in our life or due to outside influences may no longer be of interest to us. Second, of the initial desires, would I be willing to let these go for the fulfillment of their underlying desires?

For those who can't find any reason or impulse bringing them to meditate, just a sense of knowing that this is right, your time should be spent looking towards or contemplating where that knowing comes from and seeing how that knowing appears in your mind and body.

Meditation, Mind and Body

Week 2
Starting to Practice, Dealing With Thinking

So you've gotten a chance to check in to see what is motivating you to meditate. Now I'd like you to set those motivations and aims aside as we start with meditation techniques.

This simple practice is found across spiritual traditions. There are two main facets to meditative practices and the Indian traditions have two different words for them which are both often translated as "meditation" Dharana is more appropriately translated as concentration and Dhyana which can be translated as meditation or contemplation. Christian traditions often use the term contemplation or contemplative prayer for the first and meditation for the second. In Taoism the first type is regularly used in bodily practices with the second as meditative practice and as a background to the first. The practice I present here develops both of these facets.

There is also a third form of meditative practice known as Bakti (devotion) in Indian traditions or affective prayer in Judeo-Christian traditions. Because this form of meditative practice involves the worship of a deity or saint and I'd like to present a practice that doesn't require the adoption of any religious beliefs, I'm going to leave it aside here.

Let's get started. Sit down in a comfortable manner on a rug, mat, or cushion. If this isn't comfortable for you sit in a chair or on the edge of your bed. If you use a chair move forward some so that your spine is supporting the torso instead of the chair's backrest.

Gently straighten your spine. It can be helpful to imagine a thread attached to the top of the head gently pulling the head upward and simultaneously let the weight of the body flow down into the earth through your cushion. Now gently place your attention on your breath and neither encourage nor engage any thoughts that appear. Simply let them waft in and out like leaves blowing past. After some time you will notice that a stream of thought has captured your attention and you've forgotten about the breath. This moment of noticing is the real substance of this practice. When it occurs, simply place your attention on the breath and continue. Don't try to forcefully hold your attention on the breath, this will interfere with the practice and build up tension in the body. A gentle placement of the attention on the breath each time you find yourself distracted by thought is all that's needed. At these moments of noticing see also if your posture needs restoring. Thoughts can coexist with an awareness of the breath. Don't try to force the thoughts out by focusing on the breath, but develop a steady attention that continuously includes the breath.

As simple as it is, the elements of focused attention and uninvolved observation you experience through this practice are the foundation of the tremendous variety of meditative techniques that exist. While during this course you will sample some of the techniques which build upon this, it can be used for insightful investigation and transformation all by itself.

For your meditation journal, write about the one or two things which stand out the most for you from the session. It could be about the thoughts themselves or something else. Also take note of how many times you wake up to distraction and how long it is between these moments.

Meditation, Mind and Body

Week 3
Bringing Attention to the Body

This week we're going to include the sensations of the body in your practice. If needed, for learning purposes we're going to use some concentration to make bodily sensations more apparent. Usually you will meditate the same as last week and when thoughts slow down, sensations will arise in the same manner as thoughts. Treat them the same as thoughts; don't resist them and don't encourage them.

This is where a lot of people's concept of meditation is faulty. Many consider meditation to be an exercise to stop thoughts. While this is often a resulting experience from consistent practice, it is more about letting things arise without getting entangled in them. To take your practice to any depth it is important to include both the experiential elements of thought and of bodily sensations in your awareness.

This is the only change from last week...allow your attention rooted in the breath to include the sensations that arise in addition to the thoughts. If you find yourself absorbed by either a thought or sensation, bring your attention again to the breath.

Meditation, Mind and Body

This openness develops the aspect of Dhyana (meditation). Using the breath to steady the attention develops the aspect of Dharana (concentration). Bringing these to bear on both the mind and body constitutes the core practice offered here. The additional exercises that follow will start and end with this practice and require the subtlety and stability of mind that it produces in order to be effective.

Many people are particularly entangled in the thinking process, and last week's practice may not have been enough time to develop enough distance from the thinking process for bodily sensations to become noticeable. If you find this is true for you, the exercise below can be used as a way to start shifting the habitual focus of attention on thought toward the body.

Spend about half of the time you set aside for meditation using the same method as last week. When the time comes to change up, place your attention at the top of the head and feel what is there. Is it warmth? expansion? tingling? cold? tension? nothing? Take note of what you find then move down the head on all sides, including the ears, the jaw, then down the neck to the shoulders, down the arms to the fingertips, down the torso, front and back, through the pelvis and hips then down the legs to the soles of the feet and toes. Once complete, simply observe whatever thoughts or sensations arise for a few breaths then repeat the process starting from the soles of the feet. Move your attention at a pace that allows for at least two complete cycles from the crown of the head down the body and back to the crown of the head. Take note of any areas that are blind or without sensation. If you notice that you've been distracted by a thought or sensation elsewhere simply pick up where you left off.

At the end of the session let go of any effort and simply allow whatever thoughts or sensations that arise to evolve naturally without interfering.

> For your meditation journal take note of the one or two things that stand out the most to you this week and how your sessions this week differ from your sessions last week.
> Note if you are distracted more or less often this week and if you are primarily distracted by thoughts or sensations.

Meditation, Mind and Body

Week 4
Emotion & More Deeply Into the Body

Continuing from last week you should be somewhat comfortable letting thoughts and bodily sensations pass through awareness. The time between moments of waking up to distraction is likely getting shorter and you're starting to sense a stability behind the movement of the mind and the beneficial side effects of that may already be showing up in your life.

This week is not really new material, but adding a dimension to last week's practice. First, a comment about including emotion in your practice. It can be very challenging to experience emotion with the same neutrality as with thought or sensation but the idea is the same; let them flow through without encouraging or avoiding them.

Emotions can be complex and intense. If you encounter some that you have particular trouble with, break out the inner magnifying lens and look at the pieces that make them up. This will often include a cloud of thoughts, tensions, and accompanying sensations spread throughout the body conspiring to build and confirm a storyline. We get overwhelmed taking all this together, but can gain some distance by looking at the sensations and tensions as nothing more, and when the intensity has subsided, questioning the validity of the storyline and accompanying thoughts.

I'm not going to suggest a method to evoke emotion to practice with. When your practice with pure thought and sensation clears enough space emotion that needs attention will naturally arise in that space. If you have the opportunity in your day after something triggers you, take a few minutes to contemplate what comes up in this manner.

When emotion isn't arising in the space of awareness (which for most people will be the majority of the time) this week you're going to go into sensations with more detail and intricacy. This is helpful for those that find the contemplation of sensation dull or boring and will be especially enjoyable for those predisposed to body-centric activities such as dance, hatha yoga, or qigong.

Sit and observe the thoughts and sensations that arise, using the breath to steady the attention. After about half of your allotted practice time give some emphasis to the sensations that you find in the body. Look closely at the shape they take and note closely the difference in character, i.e. hot, cold, tense, tingly, vibration, heaviness or density, rigidity, etc. Use the best characterization for you, finding an idea and word that truly matches the feeling you're experiencing. Take note of any change in sensations as you place your attention on them. Note how your attention moves around as sensations dissolve, and as always, if you find yourself waking up to discover you're floating in distraction, bring your attention to the breath for a short time to steady it then dive back into the sensations.

In this practice the properties themselves aren't particularly important, but the process of examining them at this level of detail develops a worthwhile clarity and precision in the perception of the body.

> Without trying to retain, alter or eliminate them, take note in your journal of sensations that are particularly enjoyable or unpleasant and those that are particularly persistent.
> Note if the majority of sensations you experience have the same character and the share of each characteristic in your experience; for example in one session I find about half are warmth, about a quarter tingly, and the rest mostly dense.

Meditation, Mind and Body

Week 5
Beyond the Physical Body

Start from the fundamental practice of allowing the subtle objects of thought and bodily sensations to arise while steadying the mind with your breathing. After about half of your allotted time, turn your attention to the sensations of the body. Instead of focusing closely on one small portion of the body give your attention to the entire collection of sensations.

Notice how things change with nothing more than a change of attention. Notice any tendency of your attention to gravitate towards thought or a limited set of sensations in a particular area of the body. Continue like this until your attention can rest with little effort on the collection of sensations through the entire volume of the physical body rather than being drawn in by thought or a limited set of sensations. When this steadiness has been reached turn your attention to the outer edges of these sensations. This may or may not come close to the skin of the physical body. The practice is then to move the sense of feeling beyond the edge of the existing sensations. This will give more space to the sensations of the body and allow them to more easily open, evolve, and potentially to dissolve.

If you find this difficult to understand or put into practice, imagine a bubble of attention surrounding the body a few

Meditation, Mind and Body

inches outside the skin and feel the outermost sensations, then feel through the space between them and the bubble to the bubble and back again.

As you perform this practice, some symptoms of it taking hold are a peaceful sense of expansion or a direct feeling of having a body that extends beyond the edges of the physical body. It may also manifest as simply a feeling of ease and harmony in the body. Obvious examples of these will often be experienced during your meditation sessions, but watch for them to also show up without effort during your day as a byproduct of your practice.

Once this feels natural, there's no reason to keep your sense of feeling close to the body. Allow it to expand as far out as it will without effort, then contemplate the sensations that come and go without attachment. Notice when you've become absorbed in a particular group of sensations and steady your attention on the breathing for a few breaths, then breathe through the entire space of expanded feeling, returning to a position of witnessing the sensations without judgment or interference.

> The insights from this practice can often be surprising. In your meditation journal, take note of anything that you experienced in your body that is new or difficult to explain with your current idea of what your body is. If nothing from your experience matches these descriptions simply note the one or two things that stood out for you.

Week 6

Using Movement to Uncover Hidden Sensations

As you continue to observe the thoughts and sensations space will open in your experience and previously hidden physical and emotional tension will come to the surface. This organic uncovering and resolution of the knots in the mind and body is an excellent way to proceed. Sometimes however you may reach a point where the mind stills or thoughts are distant enough to be inconsequential but the body is dull, not showing any sensation or sense of space. If you find yourself in this state some gentle movements will awaken and reveal what is currently asleep in the body. I'll give some examples here but feel free to improvise. The most important point is the sensitivity and attention you bring to the movement rather than the movement itself. For this reason, most of the time it's best to move very slowly.

To start, return to the lengthening of the spine. Do this gently and not all at once. Feel the head pulled upward and as soon as a sensation or collection of sensations appears, release the lengthening and let them play out their movement and settle or dissolve before continuing. When the spine has straightened, turn your attention to the shoulders. Very slowly pull the shoulders back, releasing any unnecessary tension and again stopping when the movement has brought sensations to the surface in order to allow them to evolve then continue when they have settled or dissolved. After pulling the shoulders back move them upward, then forward, down and back again. Take note of any jerkiness in the movement and repeat the movement through those areas until it is smooth. Don't be in a hurry; if this level of attention makes for only a few shoulder rolls in the time you have, that's fine. It's the attention that you give to the movement and space you give to the resulting sensations that is important.

With the same idea, gentle movements of any part of the body help to bring out and release hidden material. Particularly fruitful areas include the neck, muscles of the face and jaw, and gentle twists of the spine. If you already have a practice such as yoga, taiji, or qigong, slowing down and repeating portions of postures or movements with this same attitude is an excellent way to deepen both practices.

Don't try to use this technique to eliminate particular tensions. The sensations that arise have their own time line and rhythm. Targeting one in order to eliminate it will only interfere with its natural unfolding often prolonging or strengthening it.

> For your journal, take note of any aversions to uncomfortable sensations that arise and what form they take, such as tensions elsewhere in the body or distractions in thought.

Week 7

More Deeply Into the Breath, Part I

We're going to change gears this week. During the first week we worked to make our motivations more clear. During the second week your practice was focused on developing some distance from thought and steadiness of the mind. In subsequent weeks we delved deeply into exploration of the body's sensations and emotion. This week and next we're going to go more deeply into the breath.

Meditate using the core practice, letting thoughts and sensations pass through with their own rhythm and bringing your attention to the breath when you find yourself distracted. Now give some extra attention to the breathing process without altering it. Note how long each in-breath is and how long before the out-breath begins. Note how long the out-breath is and how long after it completes that the in-breath begins. Is there a pause or does one breath start immediately after the other has finished? Notice how rough and noisy or fine and quiet the breathing is. Watch without interfering as the breathing changes and evolves in your gentle awareness. This is your practice for the first half of this week.

Now that you've had some practice you've probably noticed how just from your attention the breathing deepens and slows, becoming more regular and with lengthening pauses between the breaths. For the second half of the week we're going to exert some gentle control along these lines.

Sit for a time simply watching the breath as in the first half of the week. When you have settled into this, check if the lengths of the in-breath and out-breath aren't equal and lengthen the shorter of the two. Notice any change this produces in the mind and body and give some time for what arises to evolve and then settle or dissolve. When this has become comfortable and needs little to no effort to maintain, similarly check the pauses between the breaths and gently lengthen the shorter of the two until they are equal in length. Just as before, notice any changes this evokes and give them time to evolve. When this has become natural you can optionally also make the texture of the breath finer, even to the point that it is barely perceptible through sound and sensation.

Don't be in a hurry. If the entire session is just observing what is brought up by the lengthening of the shorter breath that's fine Giving these things space to resolve is most important at this point.

After intentionally adjusting the breath, It's important to relax the attention from its focus on the lengths and just watch as the breath comes and goes. After some time, if you notice the lengths have become unequal or you find yourself distracted, come back to guiding the lengths for a time.

Some interesting questions for you to consider to go more deeply into this practice; Where along the breath do particular thoughts arise and disappear? Is there anything noticeable that happens consistently at the top or bottom of the breath?

This week, during your day-to-day activities, get to know your natural pattern of breathing. It's with you every moment and has significant effects on many parts of your physiology and psychology, yet how familiar is it?

> For your journal, take note of where your attention is drawn during the practice and what comes to the surface as you continue. Note any difference in your day-to-day stress & energy levels during this week.

Meditation, Mind and Body

Week 8

More Deeply Into the Breath, Part II

Continuing from last week, when you've reached a point where it is natural and effortless to breathe with equal length breaths and pauses you're going to gently lengthen both of these starting with the length of the breaths. Note how long the breaths are and gently lengthen them by about one second. Notice how this affects the state of the body and mind. Let the thoughts and sensations that arise evolve then settle or dissolve. When this feels natural do the same with the pauses between the breaths, extending them by about half a second.

As you continue, stay close to what feels natural then lengthen when it has become natural. It is normal for the pauses between breaths to be significantly shorter than the breaths themselves and your focus should lean heavily towards the lengthening of the breaths rather than the spaces between.

If any dramatically uncomfortable thoughts or feelings appear, relax all control of the breath and simply observe. After you have given it the time it needs to evolve and settle start modifying the breath again.

> For your journal, as with last week, take note of where your attention is drawn during the practice and what appears as you continue. Note how extending the length of the breathing cycle changes your experience compared to last week.

Week 9
Where Do They Come From?

Up until now your practice has focused on letting the thoughts and sensations arise as they will without interfering, and using some techniques to help bring hidden sensations to the fore. The energy that develops with consistent practice will build a stable sense of peace and push hidden things to the surface. You may have noticed that the breathing exercises accelerated that process by energizing the body and mind.

Now that you've had time to build up some energy and stability of focus we're going to turn the attention in a subtle direction. For this practice we're going to include the thoughts, sensations, as well as the sense perceptions. We'll call all of these together subtle objects. Choose whichever naturally takes your attention; the stream of thought, the arising of feelings in the body, or the sound of your breathing.

Watch closely without effort as the object transforms then disappears. The key element to this practice is to contemplate the space in your experience where the object has disappeared and the next object spontaneously arises. You aren't looking for a position in space so much as the space or emptiness itself, the *experienced* source of the object as opposed to the *conceptual* source of the object. For example we often *conceive* of thoughts originating in the brain while in our *experience* their source is something quite different. This can be a bit difficult to express in words but with some practice it should become clear. You'll know your practice is fruitful when you hit upon a very subtle sense of sweetness or joy accompanied by a sense of creative potential. From that point all kinds of interesting experiences may arise. Remember to put your attention on the source and place of disappearance of these experiences. If you let your attention follow the experiences the energy that you've built will dissipate, leaving you attached to a dull object. While the experiences may be enticing it is the pure potential of their source which makes them so and when you stray from that it should be easy to notice the effect.

The stream of objects that you use (thought, sensation, perception) doesn't need to be the same all the time, but it's important to stay with a single object through its disappearance rather than jump from one to another.

If you find yourself resting on a sensation that is long-lived or resting in the stream of thoughts without any seeming break between them, use the sound or sensation of the breath as the object to follow to its source. Bells and chimes which have a pleasant sound that gradually fades away can also be used as an effective aide for this practice.

In your meditation journal note any changes in your experience just before and just after an object appears or disappears.

Week 10
Energy Channels in the Body

With the sensitivity to bodily sensations that you've begun to develop we're going to explore a couple facets of the body according to Indian Yoga and Chinese Qigong. The ideas they present are very similar and it's unclear if this is from ancient cultural exchange or if they examined the experience of the body and simply discovered the same details.

In both Indian and Chinese systems "subtle energies," known as Prana or Qi (pronounced "chee") respectively, flow along a network in the body much the same as blood through vessels and electrical impulses through the nervous system. In India they call these paths "nadis" and the Chinese word has regularly been translated as "meridians." Here, I'm going to simply refer to them as subtle channels. For the particularly scientific and skeptical, if the talk of subtle energies and subtle channels causes a conflict in your view of the world you can simply translate these as the subjectively experienced flow of sensations in the body...possibly even just a function of the nervous system. Regardless of how you explain the objective base of the experiences, the concept of energy flowing along channels used by these traditional systems matches very closely the subjective experiences and so are easy to recognize when then occur using this description.

Start off your practice as usual, just watching the objects arise, transform, and fade while resting the attention upon the breath. When there is some openness you're going to spend time looking closely at some particular points in the body.

Start with your attention at the perineum near the base of the spine between the anus and the sexual organs. Note any sensations at that point and nearby. Give enough attention so that they become fairly clear in their character (hot, cold, tingly, etc) and shape while still allowing them to change. Then slowly start moving the attention up the spine, feeling what is near the point of your attention. As always don't encourage or prevent any particular sensation. Continue to the top of the spine then along a line from the top of the spine across the scalp to the crown of the head. Rest here for a short time, observing the sensations there and any notable changes throughout the body while your attention rests at the crown. From there move along the scalp and down the forehead to the bridge of the nose. Drop from there down to the throat and down to the voice box. From that point it's a journey down the centerline of the front of the body.

Remember that the importance is in uncovering the sensations along the cycle, not in getting a cycle completed. When you return again to the perineum rest and observe for a time just as you did at the crown. Note the sensations at that point and any effects throughout the entirety of the body that placing your attention at the perineum has.

The channel up the spine is considered the most fundamental and what I described is the fundamental piece of this practice. As you continue and grow in sensitivity there are some things to take a look at. Notice if there are points along these channels where sensation is particularly strong and which have a consistent character which accompanies them. It's from these points, that smaller channels start to spread from these main ones.

In Indian systems the upward channel of the spine is emphasized with more than one flow of upward energy, and energy leaving the body through the crown of the head. In the Chinese system this is also of great importance but the flow of some of this energy back down the front of the body is also important and it is thought that this flow can be assisted by touching the tongue gently to the roof of the mouth.

For your practice, notice if what you experience fits these ideas of subtle channels, centers, or if touching the tongue to the roof of the mouth makes any difference as you bring your attention down the front of the body.

The additional investigations aren't necessary if you aren't drawn to explore them. If you don't find any interest in that level of detail you can continue through the entire week with the simple transit up the spine and down the front of the body examining what you find.

Some of the effects of these practices in your life can include a greater sense of energy, of not being so easily tired. Sometimes this can free up an imbalance in your body that was previously stifled, resulting in minor but noticeable physical woes that clear up after a few days. Things like slight nausea, a minor rash, or minor bouts of vertigo are nothing to be concerned with. If anything more significant presents itself or they linger for more than a few days, stop and return to the core practice detailed in weeks two & three for the remainder of this week;

you're going to need the guidance of an experienced practitioner to go more deeply into this week's practice.

> For your journal, note any strong emotions or physical sensations that consistently appear as your attention passes particular areas in the body, along with any storyline that goes along with them.

Week 11

What Am I Really?

When you have developed your practice to some extent, the openness, neutrality, and clarity may be turned towards deeper questions in life. One of the most fundamental of these questions is "What am I?" In order to know with a deep certainty the answer to that question we can't be satisfied with the second-hand answers given to us by our parents or culture. For those raised Hindu or Buddhist this would mean setting aside the idea that I'm a reincarnated soul living out one in a long history of lives. For those raised in the Christian tradition, the idea that I am a soul born from sin and which will pass into hell after death if I don't obey certain laws. For many modern people raised with a scientific perspective this will mean setting aside ideas that I'm just a collection of molecules arranged as cells in a fashion such that the organism produces thought and awareness. For most people this will include ideas such as "I'm a carpenter" or "I'm an advertising professional."

Please note that I'm not rejecting or denying any of these beliefs. I'm just asking you to look at your experience directly without looking through one of these inherited lenses.

For this practice we're going to use a very simple lens to help the mind examine the fundamental components of your experience. You're going to look directly at your own experience and see what is true rather than attach to and view your experience through beliefs. Start with the fundamental practice from weeks two & three, then simply note whether each object that arises is a thought, sensation, or sense perception. All of our experience is made up of these three in endless variation and combination along with the awareness of them. If you find something else, please let me know, I'd like to hear about your experience.

After spending some time to see this for yourself ask yourself with sincerity "What am I?" The "answer" to this question will usually be a subtle object (thought, sensation, or sense perception). Examine this object and ask yourself "If this is me, who is observing it?" For example, the result may be a thought such as "I am a Waitress." This thought appears as a concept, but you are still the seer of that concept so it can't be you, or at the very least not all of you. When this has become clear, ask yourself again what you are. In this manner you peel away false or limited ideas of what you really are, eventually leaving nothing but you in your purity. As you continue with this practice you will experience and know directly the divinity at your center with its accompanying peace, depth, clarity, strength, and imperturbability.

During this peeling away plenty of the ideas may not apply to your pure self but may be true for the circumstances of your life, such as "I am a waitress". While it may be true, it's more a description of a role; if a waitress gets fired does she stop being herself? For these there is no need to eliminate them, simply acknowledge that they have a transient truth valid for current circumstances in the world and set them aside as not your fundamental self. If they persist in your attention look deeper at the "I" they reference. It is often the case that these false senses of "I" are web-like in their formation, encompassing elements of thought and bodily sensation and need to be examined in their entirety before there is space to call out the next one by asking once again "What am I?"

In some sense this practice is more like "What am I not?" and the reason for this is that what you are can't be contained in a thought or sensation. We want to draw out the false ideas interfering with your direct experience of what you are. When you rest as that it should be clearly something very different from your experiences in the world through the senses, thoughts, and perceptions, but at the same time something very intimate and familiar, after all when are you ever away from you? A simple brief touch of this in the body or mind can spawn a number of creative, insightful, and blissful experiences. As always, if you follow the experience out it will develop but you will distance yourself from what infused the experience with creativity, insight, and bliss. Simply let them float by just as with the "ordinary" thoughts, sensations, and perceptions.

For your journal, take note of which thoughts about yourself you usually take for granted. Note also if any area of the body seems to be more "me" than others and why.

Meditation, Mind and Body

Week 12
Back to Fundamentals

This week we're going to let go of the various explorations we've taken over the past weeks and return to the foundations of all these practices; open awareness and effortless concentration. Just as described in weeks two & three, sit and simply allow the objects of experience to arise and pass away in awareness. Allow whatever appears, be it thought, sensation, emotion, or sense perception to arise and pass away in awareness. If you find yourself absorbed or distracted by a stream of subtle objects, notice that you awoke from this distraction, congratulate yourself and bring your attention to the breathing process.

There's plenty I could say about how the depth of this week's practice compares to the first few weeks', but I think it's better for you to just experience it for yourself.

> Spend some time contemplating and journaling about how your practice has evolved or changed since the first few weeks and if it provides something of value that you'd like to continue to cultivate in your life. Notice if the value that you find has anything to do with the motivations that you investigated during the first week or if this is something new in your life, something you weren't expecting.

Appendix I - Paths Forward

Now that you've completed the course, I encourage you to reflect on the practice and the various explorations you've taken over the last three months. The aim is to identify which of the weeks was most inspiring, insightful, nurturing, or peaceful for you. If you chose to keep a journal it will be helpful now as a lot has probably transpired and details may have slipped from memory. Below are some pointers for how you can continue to develop your practice, based on which week's practice you found the most fruitful.

If **weeks 1-5 or week 12** stand out for you, continue with the fundamental practice. You have a subtle sense that will allow things to blossom according to a harmonious, natural rhythm as they are ready. Don't be distracted if others have intense experiences and you don't; you're built in a way that you can receive insight quietly and without drama. Finding a meditation group to sit with regularly may be tremendously valuable for you. Give it a try.

If **week 6** stands out for you, a gentle, slow, meditative form of hatha yoga or taiji will be exceptionally valuable for you. You have a sensitivity to the body but much of its sensations are beneath the surface, and there will likely be some challenges hiding down there. A gentle form of hatha yoga or taiji will be an enjoyable, energizing, and respectful way to delve into this sensitivity. If you don't already take time to enjoy nature start making some, even if it's just a regular walk in the park.

If **weeks 7-8** stand out you should seek out an experienced pranayama teacher. If you don't know how to find one, start by asking yoga teachers you respect as yoga and pranayama are usually done together by advanced practitioners. Also don't be in a hurry. Pranayama is a powerful practice and your teacher may want you to practice yoga for some time before embarking on pranayama to ensure that your body is strong enough to handle the energies awoken without causing harm.

If **week 9** stands out you should seek a tantra teacher. A very important aside first; tantra is regularly misunderstood in the West due to a very small portion of its practices being sexually based. These practices are often touted as the essence of the tradition, but not used by most tantric traditions. Even a good teacher that is experienced in these practices may not speak of them early on. Steer clear of teachers that focus primarily on sexual practices. The practices that a good teacher for you will emphasize are those related to the direct experience of the body distinct from the physical body, and those related to the sense perceptions such as music or dance or the use of chimes and gongs.

If **week 10** stands out for you look for a teacher of kundalini yoga or qigong. These practices focus on important movements of energy through and around the body. If the upward movement was most important for you go with kundalini yoga. If the cycle up and down most captured your interest, seek a qigong teacher.

If **week 11** stood out as the most important work, you can continue your investigation using your experience directly as the sounding board for truth. This particular question is fundamental to non-dual traditions. You will likely find a great deal of insight and inspiration in traditions such as Advaita Vedanta, Chan (Zen) Buddhism, and Taoism.

To reiterate, if you don't feel drawn to these focused paths there is nothing wrong with continuing the fundamental practice. It unfolds exactly at the rhythm appropriate, bringing to attention precisely what needs to be attended to. You can fruitfully continue in this practice indefinitely. Reexamine your practice or seek a teacher/mentor if the practice becomes dull or mechanical, otherwise let the spring of freshness that flows from it be your guide.

Of course I am available for mentoring beyond this course, both for assistance in your practice and help moving through material it brings to the surface. Reach me at: MeditationCourse@JivanAmara.net

About the Author

Jivan Amara has been meditating for more than 25 years with instruction from a number of highly experienced teachers primarily from Asian traditions.

Jivan was born with the name Mathew Douglas Wiggett. Strong willed, and interested in exploring, Mathew began meditating when he was 17 in the tiny town of 2500 where he grew up.

His interest in spirituality led him to pursue a minor in comparative religious studies, where he met Professor Robert Gussner (Jina) whose approach focused on the experiential element of spiritual practices in contrast to the intellectual investigation of different religions. This element of experiencing first hand is fundamental to mystical traditions throughout the world and to the book offered here.

After graduating from college, Mathew traveled to India for four months, his first of many journeys around the world to learn from various traditions. There he took part in a variation of the Indian tradition of Sanyas (renunciation) in which he was given the name Jivan Amara, meaning immortal spirit or immortal life. On returning to the US he legally took the new name.

Jivan has lived and studied spiritual traditions in a number of places around the world; most recently Beijing & Shanghai where he furthered his study of qigong and San Diego close to Advaita teacher Francis Lucille. Jivan supports himself financially through software development. In addition to meditation, Jivan enjoys hiking, snowboarding, and playing guitar.

Made in the USA
Monee, IL
26 June 2022